It's All God, Anyway

To Martha,
Thank you for sharing
sacred space with me,
Jinks

It's All God, Anyway

Poetry for the Everyday

Jennifer (Jinks) Hoffmann

RESOURCE *Publications* · Eugene, Oregon

IT'S ALL GOD, ANYWAY
Poetry for the Everyday

Resource Publications
An Imprint of Wipf and Stock Publishers
199 W. 8th Ave., Suite 3
Eugene, OR 97401

www.wipfandstock.com

PAPERBACK ISBN: 978-1-5326-1101-8
HARDCOVER ISBN: 978-1-5326-1103-2

Manufactured in the U.S.A.   OCTOBER 11, 2016

Contents

For Alan

What Now, my Love? Listening for Mystery

Alertness is all. The call of God (through all expressions of reality) may everywhere break the veil of our daily stupor.

—Michael Fishbane

Our faithfulness (to God) is tested by the character of our responses, and by our capacity to sustain the full brunt of what occurs at any time, without sliding into simplicities or reducing the complexities.

—Michael Fishbane

"What now my Love?" I ask the Great Creator, the hidden aspect of existence. "What now?" I ask, several times a day. "Where do You want me to look? How shall I respond in this moment when I feel so dispirited by my friend's unrelenting medical crisis? How can I thank You for the love I feel for my granddaughter, Ayla, who, at almost three, has created a sentence that has seven clauses? About her pink and brown hats."

As all faith traditions teach, a spiritual life is lived in the "here and now" and not the "there and then." Thus do we experience God now. And now. And now. Or, as Rabbi David Cooper has suggested, in *God is a Verb,* God is an ongoing process of creation, a verb, not a noun. He speaks of God-ing. My life in God is here, now, alive, passionate.

In this collection of poems, written over many years, I invite you to join me as I reflect on my passion for living with the ever-increasing awareness of how all life is sacred. I will share with you the spiritual practices I favor. Spiritual practices help us awaken to reality, which is another way of naming the divine. Spiritual practices help us discern God's desire for us. My life's opus, it seems, is my attempt to awaken to reality, to God's presence. And then to be faithful to God's desire for me. Moment to moment.

The poems are stories about how I look and listen for the hidden dimension of existence. The poems tell of how, by looking and listening, I learn to love more. To have more compassion. The poems are also a map pointing me in the right direction, toward wholeness or unity, which is another way of I speak of God.

As you read the poems, I hope you will discern a deep sense of the oneness of all life. Everything is God: sunsets and a baby's death; the stillness of a mist-clad lake at dawn and a hurricane; joy and gratitude; grief and despair; kindness and "shmutz" (messy humanity).

The poems are a description of how I walk into the fire, not away from it. I walk toward the fire of my unconscious, unhealed wounds. I walk toward the fire of the wild, brute, impersonal darkness of life's unpredictability. The fire is also the fire of transformation and healing— the healing of beauty, of love, of God. The healing offered by mystery. The healing offered by turning and facing, over and over, my shmutz.

This is that collection—a record of my relationship with the divine, in the everyday and the ordinary. The poems are of, from, and to the Great Creator.

Consciousness. Choice. Kindness.

To paraphrase the Swiss psychiatrist Carl Jung, life goes better with consciousness. I am to look, to be aware, to engage creatively with what reality offers. Moment to moment. The Source of Life, great unnameable mystery, creates existence anew continuously, revealing both heart-opening beauty and wild, unpredictable darkness to our eyes, ears, and senses. If I am awake, I will experience radical awe and wonder, or radical dread and sorrow in response to Life's creation of life. My intention is to be radically attuned to life's sacredness.

I am to listen to the guidance I receive from the divine, through my dreams, my reading and writing, the joys and difficulties of my life. The invitation is to become more God-minded, more conscious of divinity through my few accomplishments, but even more through the messes

I make. I am being guided at all times to become whole, to know and claim all aspects of who I am, to make conscious choices.

I have been looking for and listening to the divine for forty years. This has helped me become more loving. At least some of the time. More compassionate. The more I am awake to the reality that is God, and the more I heed what I am being asked by life to do, the kinder I become. To others, to myself, and to our earth. I become stronger, more authentic, and more natural. More reverent. And more irreverent.

Spiritual Practices

In the 40 or so years I have been engaged in conscious spiritual practice, I have discerned some of the ways I am guided. Wholeness is the means and the end of a life well-lived. Neurosis has been described as the discrepancy between the self-image and the Self. So the Holiness that is God sends daily and sometimes frenetic missives to help us move towards our wholeness, our holiness. This is the process of healing.

A deep call to wholeness issues from my dreams, which are one type of objective communication I receive on a regular basis, for they issue from my unconscious. My conscious mind can play all sorts of tricks, but dreams tell me truths that are often difficult and painful. Occasionally the dreams say "Good work. You're on track. Rest a little." But more often they are some version of God sighing in loving exasperation. I am fortunate to remember messages received, almost every night. Sometimes the dreams are practical and clear, so I understand what I'm being asked to do. I dream of a friend who has been less than usually communicative, and discover, upon calling, she is in a mild state of depression. Frequently, though, the night missives make no sense to me. It is only when I sit contemplatively with them for some time, or when one of my spiritual directors or my Jungian analyst assists me, that I understand the call to healing and wholeness. I cannot see my own back.

There is nothing that is not the divine. It was another dream that told me "it's all God anyway." My dreams know much more than I do. Reality is God. Because of our limitations, we perceive of ourselves as being separate, but there is a unity. A Oneness. Joy and sorrow, elation and suffering, evil and goodness, the deer and the leopard, even grass-blades and flies.

Perhaps my primary spiritual practice is engaging with and learning from my dreams. Jung spoke of Big Dreams. Dreams that are so remarkable they can change our perspective on life. Big Dreams are usually remembered forever.

Dream: I walk into a room. I am unusually awake. I think "this is God." I feel terror. I feel awe. I think "this is unity."

For some time, I have felt compelled to honor this archetypal dream of the unity of the divine. It is a dream I will mine for wisdom all of my life. The following collection of poems, written over many years, depicts my journey in making meaning of this remarkable dream. All life, or God, or reality, is unity. There is no reality that is only light or dark, though it certainly can feel that way at times. While intellectually I have held this perspective of "both/and" for years, the dream somehow speaks to a deeper spiritual and existential truth. The dream addresses the overwhelming terror and awe I might feel if I were to encounter the divine. I know this is not possible. Life itself is terrifying and awesome. Abraham Joshua Heschel invites us to live with radical amazement. Knowing we have so little real control, and yet choosing to stay radically awake to the glory as well as the terror of life, is the sacred invitation. We are always just one breath away from death.

My life is my spiritual practice. I have a keen sense of the movement of spirit in my everyday world, so I'm particularly attentive to the places in my days and nights where I feel shmutzy, or messy, out of alignment, disgruntled, stirred. Shmutz cleaning is an incomparable consciousness raiser. God is surely trying to get my attention at these times.

The wisdom of the universe has been "individuating me" all my life, sometimes with my cooperation and awareness, more often by dragging me, kicking and screaming, to where my soul knows I need to go. Individuation, a term coined by Jung, is the process of integrating all aspects of ourselves and of coming more and more into relation with the Self, which is a Jungian term for the Godhead or the divine. Individuation is the process of becoming whole. This means all parts of ourselves: both the less-than-attractive aspects and the more wonderful and shining parts of which we are not aware. This is sometimes called dark and bright Shadow. Individuation means becoming the person we were created to be. This is a lifetime's work.

The love I feel for the Holy One of All Being is impossible to articulate, but I never cease trying. I am in love with God despite life's challenges; indeed, maybe even because of them. There is hardly a day when I do not celebrate the miracle of life. Working open-heartedly with life's darkness can awaken us. In my case, it is mostly "bread-and-butter darkness," although some painful periods of my life have had me on my knees. Despite this, many of my poems are shot through with love and spirit. They are my attempt to say something about my obsession and my sense of deep connection to the ineffable, to mystery. I once said to my poetry mentor: "Jason, all I ever write has something to do with the mystery of life, the divine. Should I try and write a variety of different poems?" He groaned and said, "For God's sake, no. We all write about our obsessions." It seems that our obsessions are another calling card of the divine.

In addition to writing poetry and reflecting on the sacred messages being revealed in my dreams, I also read spiritual material daily. I'm particularly interested in Jewish theology and mysticism, Kabbalah, Jungian psychology, and Buddhist thinking. There are times when I have felt a bodily sense of Presence as I read. Some word or phrase or idea is suddenly numinous, and I find myself in tears. It's as if there is some subliminal commandment which directs me: "Stop right here. Ponder on what you have just read." This will frequently take me to where a poem decides to "come through." My poems "just arrive," and although I am certainly awake and present in the process of writing, I do feel somewhat written through. This is why I'm often in love with my poems. My poems help me wake up. Like my dreams, they are instruments in the hands of the Holy One to raise my consciousness of mystery. Poems are another of God's ways of talking with me. Sometimes my listening is a bit off, and I write what we affectionately call drek (rubbish in Yiddish.) Either this or the Muse's muse is AWOL that day. When I pray aloud, in the spiritual direction sessions I offer, I have a similar experience of being prayed through.

Another spiritual practice is a daily walk, wherever I am. A walking meditation where I pray for always increasing consciousness, choice, and kindness. In Florida, our winter home, I walk for one to two hours every day, no matter the weather. Only thunder, lightning, or pelting rain keep me away from this time with God. What a privilege.

Etty Hillesum, a young Dutch woman who died at Auschwitz, believed her relationship with the divine resided in her capacity to see the truth, to bear it, and to find consolation in it. She recognized a deep indwelling, and said something like "I speak of that deepest place within me, which for convenience's sake, I call 'God'." I'm with Etty. She was remarkable in her capacity to seek light and beauty, even in a situation that surely was overwhelmingly dark and evil. As a child, I read her diary and letters, *An Interrupted Life*. Etty has been with me since then, as inspiration.

My daily journaling helps me intuit God's presence and guidance. I journal about those aspects of the preceding day or days which moved me either to joy or sorrow. I journal about my conflict. I journal about my overwhelming gratitude for my awareness of breath entering and leaving; God's breath within. No effort on my part. I journal about how a tiny purple weed, growing in the thick tufts of grass outside my home, says "Stop. I am perfect. See me." I journal about my conversation on the beach with the man who fishes daily. He throws everything back. "I just like being quiet," he says. About how his crooked smile and slightly stained teeth suddenly make me want to howl—an ecstatic flash of unthinkable intimacy has just occurred; a knowing that he, too, is God. I journal about the caesural feelings that arrive at times, a simultaneous grief and ecstasy in response to "nothing special," that make me feel I have just awakened.

I see my journaling as a kind of psychospiritual analysis with God. I write and write, and God listens. I kind of "hear" the elemental "uh-huh." And then I listen more deeply to myself and something gets lifted up to reflect on.

These spiritual practices help me in my lifelong jouney towards wholeness.

An Invitation

The divine has a unique language for each of us. Our spiritual imperative is to discover the language with which the Great Creator addresses us. When we do, we can get on with the business of being awake to life's extraordinary unfolding in every single moment; we can be brought into alignment with how we are meant to live our lives, both for the long term and from moment to moment. When we listen to God, we can do our deep psychospiritual work, which helps us individuate, helps us live with more meaning, purpose, and deliciousness, even if we will often be rooting around in the muck.

My hope is that in companioning me on my journey you will find more of the unique language that the divine has for you. The Holy One has innumerable ways of inviting us closer, of singing to us.

As you read of how I experience life through connection, I invite you to notice how your relationship with the divine is real, alive, and intimate. My Love, as I keep saying, invites me into the consciousness of the Something Bigger without and within. The silence that blesses me when I leave the realm of dreams in the early morning is especially numinous. In that liminal space my first awareness is frequently my love for my huge family; my husband, three remarkable sons and their wonderful wives, eighteen grandchildren, and seven great-grands. And counting. A felt love that just arrives. My Love invites me to stand firm in my witness—of trees torn from their roots by the wild weather we humans have had a part in creating, of the pain friends or family may suffer. Perhaps you will notice that you have been thinking a lot about simple paintings, or sand-art? Is the divine inviting you to grow in your creative expression? Are you dreaming a great deal about your grandmother? What is the invitation in the dreams? We are all invited by divinity to honour our existence, to be real, to be who-we-are, to see our life as it is, not how we'd like it to be. The guidance is for us to be awake and present, with much kindness and compassion, for ourselves and for others.

I also invite you to notice the role of life-giving darkness. It is from darkness and the unknown that new life emerges, the "dark room" or womb in which creation gestates. This is the darkness of infinite possibility, rich, fertile, inviting; a darkness which is the springboard for life. This darkness, called the "fertile void" in Gestalt theory, invites and allows pregnancy, birth, creation. I know this darkness too. It can feel frightening. It can also sometimes feel like gently encompassing velvet. This is not the terror of which the dream speaks.

So why did I receive the dream of walking into a room? Dreams come to teach us what we don't know. Dreams always come in the service of healing and wholeness. Why the unshakeable belief that these poems have to be presented in relationship with this remarkable, archetypal dream? Why the passion to share with you, the reader, some of my spiritual goals and spiritual practices, and how I attempt to accomplish them?

I am an elder, as we seventy-plus people are called. My life is rich and multi-layered, spirited, vibrant. I am profoundly grateful to feel guided in these ways. This is my attempt to share with you some of the gifts I have received over the years; some of my insights about being awake to life's mysteries and the paradox at the heart of soul. I want to invite you to deepen your own covenant with life, to become more faithful to your own soul's calling. I am alive with the passion for sacred awakening. I want to share this divine obsession with you.

Also, I know I am being obedient, as well as I can discern, to the commandments I have received from the Holy One of All Being: share your writings with others in a book. Put your poetry together. Use this dream as a springboard.

So, dear reader, here are my poems, on the dark, the light, and the unity of my life. Please companion me as I walk my days, as I ponder tragedy and grace, ecstasy and dread. Celebrate my version of mysticism with me, my obsession with Mystery. Sit with me as I work on myself and as I listen for the Source of Life with the people who honour me in seeking spiritual direction. Meet some of my friends, my beloved husband, my three sons and their wives, and some of my eighteen grandchildren. Celebrate my enormous love for Alan, and nod in acknowledgement of how he is also the bane of my life. Marriage and relationships are fine instruments of individuation. Join me in my exquisite compassion for our humanity, for the ordinary messes which trip us daily. We are each simply a *bombu*, with our foolish, mortal, so-human longings, as the Japanese Buddhist term teaches us lovingly. And finally, rest with me in my tradition of Judaism, where I honor my roots, I'dor vador, from generation to generation.

Section 1:
A Way of Being in the World

Melody of the Ocean

The *quiet*.

Only an occasional sound.
A passing boat hums.
A car door slams.
The cawing of a hungry bird.

You can almost hear the waves,
singing one at a time to the ocean.
You might even think
you hear a *niggun**, this almost
inaudible song to the universe.

Pause even briefly;
you may hear the sound
of your blood loving you,
your heart, the part
that sings, beating
a soft tattoo.

* Jewish religious tune or melody

Rachmaninov and the Elephant

Sixteen years old. I hear
   Rachmaninov's Second Symphony,
     third movement.

My heart suddenly knows.

No-one ever speaks
   of the sacred.

In my purple-and-white checked
    school uniform
       I keep looking over my shoulder

trying to catch the Shadow
    tracking me,
       the boundary

where visible and invisible
    dissolve.

But all I see
        is giggling schoolgirls.

Fast-forward too many years.
     Like the blind man and the elephant,
       my hands like Marcel Marceau's,
         I pat space, seeking answers.

I cannot cease exploring.
     Like T. S. Eliot I keep ending
      at the beginning.

Unlike T. S. Eliot, I know less.

I know, at least, that I will never know
        the elephant, but I cannot keep out
            of that room, where I touch
                and pat.

I cannot stop believing that the skin
        of the elephant warms
            to my touch. I cannot stop
                yearning for celestial music.

Jennifer (Jinks) Hoffmann

The Rush of Mystery

The air is vengeful
despite the radiant sky.
Normally placid sea curls
have become fiery jumpers,
and rush menacingly
towards today's few walkers.

There are not many
as faithful as I.

How can I love
only when life is gentle?

Today the rush of Mystery
frightens a little,
asks for steady feet
on bone-chilling sand,
against gale-like winds.
We regulars have abandoned
our hats.

Leaving our heads bare
feels almost sacred today.

December 14th, 2012

It's like this sometimes.
You wade through swampy lagoon
up to your thighs, quietly,

so as not to disturb
the Great Blue Heron
meditating, graceful as

Jacob's ladder reaching
heavenwards. Mullet and lady-fish
leap, positively inches

out of the water. The invincible scrub
between the sucking lagoon
and white beach-sand

entices. Only minutes
later, on Hideaway Beach,
a school of dolphin—six

at least—break the unusual stillness
of the ocean's surface
with occasional sassy tail-flips.

Just three small boats,
a few fishermen, no radio, no beer,
pelicans dive-bombing

their frightened prey, and the sun,
radiant, cheerful, saying yes to all.
On the way back to Tigertail Beach,

Jennifer (Jinks) Hoffmann

hundreds of side-scuttling sand crabs
the advance guard, clearing
your path. The Heron has been joined

by his white cousin. Both solemn,
regal. The flying fish are gone.
The tide has changed.

In the hot car you turn on the radio,
just to hear the time. The announcer's voice
telegraphs urgency. Breaking

news is of a school
                    in Newtown,
                              Connecticut.

Portrait of the Heart in Darkness

There is a place beyond
light's steady breath
where all that is possible
is to hold
the impossible.

A mother with wild eyes
and empty breasts
sits silently
on sun-baked
Saharan earth.

A father hears words
he has been dreading,
and fights tears
and empty pockets
on the grimy bus ride home.

A child watches her brother
laced with tubes
and machines,
pale against white sheets,
and asks *why?*

There is a place
where all that is possible
is to hold the impossible.

Jennifer (Jinks) Hoffmann

Here, life asks only
that we place one foot
in front of the other,
that we make the bed,
that we wash the dishes.
Here, life demands
witness, demands
that we turn
towards the darkness
of the heart, demands
that we breathe
in unison
with the impossible.

Only then we may create
that place where Mystery
may blow gently
on the embers
of barely breathing coals.

Raising the Sparks

The world is having a dream about itself.
Your job is to find out what the world is trying to be.
—Robert Sardello

It could be as simple
as using a good paring knife
and singing, as you peel the apple

from top to bottom, then kissing
your grandson's nose as you drop
the unbroken peel on his head.

It could be checking the herbs
in the outdoor pots, noticing
the basil needs water.

It could be wrapping yourself
in a prayer shawl, fingering your beads,
studying the Bible — all the better
to empty the space, prepare the ground
for the silence which offers answers
to questions which never cease.

It could be putting on your hat,
your boots and your gloves
and shovelling Mrs. Cohen's walkway

before you drive her to the doctor.
You wish she would talk less,
but you tuck your impatience

into the pocket of your coat,
and it escapes only once.
It could be as simple as blessing

the newspaper as you open it,
praying for the spoiled and lost ones
on all corners of the earth.

It could be as simple as knowing
that prayer is also love-in-action
or even hate in non-action,

that there is only one you
in the entire universe,
that your spark-raising cannot be done
by anyone else, not even by God.

Reality

*I respond to reality in such a way that I look on existence as a great
mystery… at certain moments this mystery carries such a strong
charge… it points toward a greater context, one that is
incomprehensible to our normal everyday reason.*
Although it begins in something very concrete.

—Tomas Tranströmer

There is no warning.
It doesn't have to be
a red-laced sunset

or even searing lightning
tearing open the blackness.
It can be someone

frowning, or a stale
piece of bread, even a song
that irritates you.

There are times,
if you acquiesce to life,
that you know
that you don't know.

And for some reason
this brings a lump
to your throat.

Theology

*Theology is…a 'speaking about God' out of the thickness
of human experience, through the vitalities of one's breath and body
in the course of life, on the way to death.*

—Michael Fishbane

My study today is bearing witness
to the explosion of Saucer Magnolias,
pink and white, transforming the neighbourhood
overnight into a wedding party;
blue and white crocuses and tiny yellow narcissus,
whose patience through the long winter
has been rewarded. I even saw
three trillium triumphing their way
from exultant soil.

Everybody is out today.
Tank tops and tiny shorts on winter weary legs,
baseball hats worn backwards.
The foreman of the construction crew on Melrose
whistles cheerfully and calls to Joe to move his ass.
The ice cream store on the corner
of Fairlawn and Avenue has opened, outdoor tables
occupied by teens talking loudly while consulting iPhones.
Starbucks too, has not one sunny seat available;
the metal bowls of water for the dogs need refilling.
I see an elderly man on Cranbrooke
stooped over his scraggly bed of rose bushes.
He clips the surrounding grass
with what looks to be a pair of nail scissors.
The greenness looks artificial. He turns and frowns
as I carol *good morning.* Perhaps he was meditating,
one blade at a time.

I am studying God as I walk, my seventy plus body
not as sturdy as it was. When I turn around
too fast, to admire twins on the swings,
to chat with their Filipina nanny, I lose
my footing some. My skin has become paper thin,
and sometimes blossoms of tiny bruises make a grand design.
When I show these to my grandchildren
and ask them to make interpretations
of the patterns, they giggle.

I stop for a while. The clouds seem to pattern
some elemental teaching
about the ten-thousand lives we live
in any one moment.
My breath thickens.

Jennifer (Jinks) Hoffmann

A Bird on a Bicycle

Contemplation is a long, loving look
at the real.
                        —Walter Burghardt

Seventy-three. Nearly.
My wrists bird-like
because of incipient osteoporosis.

I am bemused by the creaks
and cracks and colours
of my body. Bruises a fine shade
of purple. How firm and fine I used to be.
Breasts like upturned peaches.
With a cherry in the right place.
Thighs that could hold their own.
A definitive waistline.

My old woman in purple says
somethin' like, Babe,
it's downhill from here. Enjoy
what you got now.

I refuse to stop riding
my ancient bicycle
around the aging neighbourhood.

I pray sometimes;
not to *God-God,* mind you,
but to my own mindfulness.

Careful. And. You go, girl.
I've been hangin' out
with God forever.

I feel a bit like Etty Hillesum
who said something like
I speak of that deepest place
within me, which for convenience
sake, I call God.

As for me, the longer I hang,
the less I know God.

I think of Alan as I wobble on the bike,
and feel a bit like Ogden Nash
who said somethin' like
To keep your marriage brimming,
With love in the loving cup,
Whenever you're wrong, admit it;
Whenever you're right, shut up.

I feel a bit like a bird trying
to ride a bicycle, belting out
an *Etta James,* who said somethin' like
A lotta people think the blues is depressin',
but that's not the blues I'm singin'.
When I'm singin' blues, I'm singin' life.
People that can't stand to listen to the blues,
they gotta be phonies.

Jennifer (Jinks) Hoffmann

A Feather

So vulnerable. A feather
on a breath of down-wind.

If we really know
we could be snuffed out
in an instant−
just like that−
could we too,
be borne
on gentle drifts of air,

random currents
moving us through life?

I hear birds in the garden;
they have not yet flown South.

Sunlight filters through the slats,
our new faux-wood window-blinds.

A fire-engine screams
on Bathurst. And then fades.

I pray quickly
for all concerned
and then attend again
to drifting on the breath
of down-wind.

Surgery later today.

If I really know
I could be snuffed out
just like that,
would I glory in bird-song
and filtered sunshine
that speak of sweet, lazy days?

I turn once more
to becoming
the feather.

Section 2:
Mysticism

Everything and Everyone

(The divine) is just now, just here, just always.
                        —Michael Fishbane

Again. It happens again.
You're walking the beach.
You're faithful. This, after all,
is spiritual practice. It's an unfriendly
day, where gusty gulps of wind grab
your blue baseball hat,
turn it backwards.
You cannot find one
clear section of sand, so keep
stepping on sharp shell shards,
more nasty and pointed
than usual.

It all feels off. And still there are
moments when you are spun
around wildly. Something
other has called. Again.

Everything seems the same.
Nothing seems the same.

You long, with an ache
that could tear the heart
out of an athlete, to tell
someone—it's happened again.

It's just the divine doing
what the divine does—
but the God-pumps of life
are tearing your heart open.

Jennifer (Jinks) Hoffmann

People will say
what are you talking about?
You will want to say
something about love,
but how can you explain?

Your friend Anna, who you could
scarcely love more; the odd man
who walks the length of the beach
every single day, trawling
his metal detector—faithful, too,
in today's wildness;
a father yelling meanly
at his boy who keeps
running at the shore birds.

Everything. Everyone.
Even the shell shards;
you even love the shell shards.

The Same Thing

Every now and then
she is able to leave
her old grey coat behind.

She walks in the neighbourhood,
humming tunelessly;
notices the air singing
to the insides of her wrists,
and the surprisingly loud
rat-tat-tat of the woodpecker.
Rhythm section.

On these days, everything
brings her to tears;
not just the violin section
of August cicadas,

or the blushing of the straggling roses
in the park on the corner;
not just the old man struggling
to put the lid on his container
at Second Cup, or the dark-roast
smell of coffee.

Not just the single dimple
on the right cheek of the checkout
girl at Metro, or the obvious pride
of the young man rearranging
summer peaches.
She wonders if she is foolish
to feel such moist gratitude,
but decides she isn't. Rather, it's as if

she and the air and the woodpecker
and the cicadas and the roses and the old man
and the coffee and the girl with the dimple
and the young man and the peaches
are all part of the same thing.

Just Everything Slowing

Our faith does not cause us
to see different things,
but to see things differently.
        —Teilhard de Chardin

How can we possibly realize
in our hearts,
in our lives,
the Tree of Life is burning
without being consumed,
unless we linger?

Mystery only reveals itself
if we look long enough,
if we listen.

You see, the world, inside and out,
is on fire with divinity,
but we cannot see this,
if we slipstream our days.

Abraham Joshua Heschel says
stay with things long enough
to sense the ultimate
in the ordinary.

Thus inspired this early morning, I sit.
Flutter my eyes closed, butterfly wings.
Brush my cheeks with fingertips,
and listen.

Jennifer (Jinks) Hoffmann

Construction nearby.
A saw whines on and off, ending
with a petulant whistle.
I am tired, despite ample sleep.
Squirrels chase one another irritably
up and down the Norway Maple
at the end of the garden.
Time passes. My bum hurts.
How long have I been sitting?
Where is the promised Eden,
in this moment?

I flutter my eyes shut again.
Listen in and out.
Once, twice, three times.
Nothing.

And then.
There is a lushness.
I can sense it.
A tear begins its descent;
my breath begins a soft humming.
Everything slows.
Not rainbows and marching bands,
not angels and hallelujahs.
Just a lushness,

and everything slowing.

The Empty Room

In Ayn Sof *...everything hidden and visible meet, and (this is) the root of both faith and unbelief.

—Azriel of Gerona

Billy Collins says that the poet looks out
the window and knows, like the chef
looks down at the chopping board and garlic.

Like Billy I look and listen. Today
it's the sound of a single bird,
the screech of car tires around a corner.

Today it is a phone-call from my son,
the learning of the sudden death
of my friend, the aroma of roasted garlic.

I know something when my breath
quickens. Or slows. When I have tears
that are big enough to hold my roots.

My breath whispers the name
that cannot be said. Mystics suggest
that the Source of Being

has at its center an empty throne
in an empty room. Life offers this, now.
All there is to do is bow,

nose to the ground; hold the questions,
hold the faith, hold the unbelief;
listen and look and breathe.

29

Jennifer (Jinks) Hoffmann

It is here, where the hidden and visible
meet, the place where contradictions
gambol like lion and lamb;

it is here that faith and unbelief
turn to one another
and take marriage vows.

This is the place in which Steve Jobs
must have found himself just before he died.
His sister Mona tells that all he said was
Oh wow! Oh wow! Oh wow!

* Ayn Sof without end, limitless one. Kabbalistic term for the divine.
**** Azriel of Gerona: A 13th century Kabbalist who was a student of
Isaac the Blind.*

Just When I Think

The racket has started again,
just when I think
the construction
on the house directly behind,
has ceased.
It's like that.

Just when I think I know—

Peace, I think, hello God.
Wriggle more deeply
under the bedcovers.
I can now open
to universal wisdom,
I think, and wriggle
some more.

And then the decibel-laden
twin roars of jack hammer
and whining blade through concrete
recur. Spitefully.

I think I know—

Jennifer (Jinks) Hoffmann

The catfish doesn't think
it knows the ocean.
The fledgling cricket creeping
on dewy summer grass
just creeps.
Picasso lets the canvas
tell him; Mozart,
the flute. What hubris
to think I'm awake
to the makings of any
moment.

Since I was sixteen, when
I first discovered thought,
I keep making
the same mistake;
perhaps at eighty-three
I'll know
I don't know
anything,
and will finally
relax into jack-hammers
and whining saws.

A Rabbit from a Hat

It is late.
I am tired.
The demand is imperative:
go for a walk.
I try to bargain.
Go.
Clearly, I have no choice.
I leave the house yawning.

That something-within
which has its way with me,
sometimes pleasantly,
sometimes not,
has triumphed again.

Five minutes later I am inhaling
the freshness of Spring lilac
on the cusp of full bloom.
The cool air, relieved
of the humidity
of the past two days,
caresses my cheeks.

I watch the neighbourhood
slow as I do; my walk
has become prayer.

Jennifer (Jinks) Hoffmann

Just moments before I am home,
I see the rabbit which appears
to have adopted Brookdale Avenue.
It freezes on our neighbour's lawn,
then begins to scamper away, in fright.
I speak softly: *wait God,* I say,
there is nothing to fear. Wait. please.
And God stops. Inquisitive.
Bright brown eyes.
Inquisitive. I stop.
Bright green eyes.

The moment is imperative.

A Love Poem to God

My eye kept telling me "something is missing from all I see."
So I went in search of the cure.
The cure for me was (God's) beauty,
the remedy...to love.

—Rabia of Basra
(Female Islamic saint and a central figure in the Sufi tradition.)

God, may I tell You
what I see now?

The ocean is striped:
alternating ribbons
of turquoise and navy-blue.
Seersucker puckers of waves.

A red kayak close
to shore—the two women
do not paddle in unison;
they are laughing too much.

Three white caps seek
the horizon, which today
is a wedding band of teal:
my favourite colour.

Fat momma clouds
and their babies dart
across a winged sky.
A loan pelican soars.
Why do I stop myself
from loving You
as much as my heart
wants me to?

Jennifer (Jinks) Hoffmann

Why do I turn
toward shadow
when the sun beckons
with ultimate kindness?

God, help me not bind
myself with ideas
about You, help me not
shut You out with readings

and chanting; help me simply
look and see, so I may fall
into a million pieces
of love.

Psalm 42 at 2 a.m.

Dream: I walk into a room. I am suddenly unusually awake.
I think this is God. I feel terror. I feel awe.
I think this is Unity.

One day a leopard came stalking into the synagogue, roaring and
lashing its tail.
Three weeks later, it had become part of the liturgy.

—Franz Kafka

A longing
to be as still
as a deer, head
tilted, nostrils flared,
scouring
the surroundings
for water or danger;
a longing to peer
into the very air
to see if the contours
of the mystery
will be revealed;
a longing to touch
something other
than the loneliness
of our own
hand.

Jennifer (Jinks) Hoffmann

And still we fill
the space
with manicured
lawns, trimmed hedges,
plans on when to roast
the chicken,
annoyance at wilted salad,
and would pears do
for dessert?

What of the moment
when deep calls to deep,
the moment when,
if we listen just
that fraction longer,
we may hear
the song sung
only at night?
What if we dare
look more carefully
for that which is almost
hidden?
We might see
the deer snorting,
a puff of vapour
escaping
into the very air;
we may hear
the trembling creature
stamping her hoof
on dew-laden grass,
then lapping,
in last rites,
from a pool
which reflects nothing.
Perhaps tears
will be our food
as we witness

the deer
sighing, turning
in the moonlight,
surrendering her throat
to the leopard's
sudden fangs.

The Cycle

What a blow to discover
that exile and redemption
are eternally contemporary and ongoing.
I want no more Egypt. I want Holy Land forever.

I want a God of supreme love, pure and gentle kindness,
who rewards my good behaviour in a manner
eternally contemporary and ongoing.
A kind of Mr. Rogers.

Instead I discover, to my excitement and disappointment,
my God is a kind of Leonard Cohen.
Raspy voiced, sexy, unfaithful, creative, disdainful, furious.
Gorgeous and utterly compelling.
I grumble, complain and whine
like my ancestors,
about this God who journeys with me.

I want a God of supreme love, pure and gentle kindness,
a kind of Mother Teresa, who despite her experience
of the felt absence of God's love,
devoted her life
to tending those in the world's underbelly.

Instead I discover, to my excitement and disappointment
my God is a kind of Judith Viorst.
Prolific, funny, a self-acknowledged hedonist,
she blithely uses her very own family
for her prodigious creative literary material,
and insists at all times,
on valet parking and 5 star hotels!

God erases the God of my longing
with a careless sweep of hand,
and with a sexy, raspy voice,
invites me into the reality
that exile and redemption
are eternally contemporary and ongoing.

Do you think it's such fun for me?
God grumbles throatily, pouring a single-malt Scotch
and turning up Thelonious Monk on the ipod.

A Football as Instrument of Spiritual Transformation

In her late sixties she becomes allergic
to *holy-holy.* On a rampage she donates
six large boxes of spiritual books to Goodwill;
tears the *I* page from her Oxford Concise,
where mother had underlined
the word *improvement.*
She ceases meditating, either in the sitting
or walking state, and shudders
every time someone uses the word *mindful.*
No-mind, emptiness and stillness become curse words.
In a fit of pique, she unsubscribes to every
spiritual or health or self-improvement mailing list,
and signs up for travel, food and wine updates,
and the *New York Times Book Review.*

Still. Wisdom has her way,
natters to her, relentlessly:

Eternity in a grain of sand.
The universal in the particular.
All is impermanent. Any clutching at the past
or the future is based on illusion.
There is only the present moment.
God is Love. God is breath. God is No-Thing.
God is the manifestation of Energy in the world.
God is the balance between lovingkindness and firmness.
Guidance towards wholeness issues from the unconscious.
The dream has all the knowledge you need.
All is One.
She remembers what Jung would have called
a Big Dream, which occurred some years ago when spiritual life
was disappearing for the hundredth time:

You are rowing alone to an island. On God's holy day. The 13th.
To plant seeds of uncertainty and unknowing.
She didn't understand it then.
She doesn't understand it now.

She tosses a massive pile of journals
into the storage room in the basement;
a fire, she thinks, when winter arrives.

Arrrgh. She feels like Lucy.
Looks around cannily for a football
to snatch from some hapless Charlie Brown.

Jennifer (Jinks) Hoffmann

It's Just Plain Good

Sometimes it's just plain good.
Skies that remain blue
all day, the temperature just right,
the air soft. Low tide; there is ample space
to walk on satiny sand.
None of the prodigious number
of shells get underfoot as I walk in a reverie.
I have taken to humming.
Melodies arrive of their own accord;
I couldn't replicate them if I tried.
They are of the moment,
like today's goodness.
It's easy to see gratitude
written in the sand, to smile
radiantly at the few regulars
who seek God on their beach walk.
Do they know they seek God?
Blatant evidence is everywhere today.
The flock of Royal Terns allow me
to walk in their midst without
taking to flight. A little girl, about three or four,
wearing a red bathing-suit
and a red bow in her brown curls,
pats a small pile of sand.
She talks gravely to herself.
The water is turquoise;
I see the black and white
sheephead swimming close.
Palm trees shade some
of the tall buildings.
I smell frangipani blossoms—
they seem early this year.
The unanticipated quiet shimmers.

I find God everywhere today.
But when it's just plain good
I could find God
in a toothpick.

A Perilous Path

The spiritual life walks a perilous path
through the howl of evil and emptiness....
confronting its terrors....
without denials or evasions.
                                            —Michael Fishbane

Like the Roadrunner
we race to the edge
of the cliff

pedaling furiously
in mid-air
as we hold

to the illusion
there is no abyss.
This seems preferable

to running
smack-dab into
a brick wall.

But is it?

We imagine if we run
faster, work
harder, or think

deeper, we will
understand, even
manage reality.

We keep forgetting.

We are only
one comma
in the story

with no beginning
and no end.

Section 3:
The Work

A Poem

A poem is a hand, a hook, a prayer.
It is soul in action.
Poets compose in a frenzy of ecstatic intuition.
—Edward Hirsch

Your hand, Your hook.
My prayer.

Help me recall
what my heart knows
but has forgotten,
as the rocks on the river-bed
rattle me, as my words are muted
by the miracle of morning light.

Help me reach
for my shield and my staff,
pen and paper,
my voice of soul.

Words are the thread
to the invisible heart.
Who is the author?

Reveal to me
once more
the thin place inside time
where talking and listening become One,

as, in a blaze
of intuition,

Jennifer (Jinks) Hoffmann

I remember

my first tongue,
the language I spoke
before I was born.

Help me re-discover
as Rainer Maria Rilke offers,
that You are the Other
in my solitude,
a silent center
for my conversations with
myself.

The Chase

If you are a poet...you will always be chasing a way to write...
In the world of imagination, all things belong.
If you take that on faith,
you may be foolish. But foolish like a trout.

—Richard Hugo

...and although they tell you
the thrill is in the chase,
don't believe it.

The thrill comes if you ever corner
a word with lush, thick eyelashes,
and are able to nail it to the page
with your mascara, which you've had
since your third child was born.
He is now forty.
You didn't use the mascara once.

Short sentences, they say.
Images that bring you to climax,
quickly. Or slowly. Depending
on whether you believe in God.

You often feel as if you are
on your way to the gallows,
the torture of wanting a poem
so musical, it boasts words
like *mellifluous*, and *garrulous*--
although you know
only single syllable words
should be used in any writing
worthy of the name poem.

You hunger to create something
that sings with your wisdom,
dances with rhythm ripe
with revelation, and uses
the tambourine salaciously.
Don't use long sentences. Or words
like *revelation*. Or *salaciously*.

It's a fool's game, I tell you,
but one you are condemned
to play until your mind enters
a retirement home, your mouth
shouts *Eureka*, or your body drops
like a stone on the way to heaven.
Whichever comes first.

One Line

I want to write
one line
of poetry
perfect
for this moment,

sanctifying the pen
sanctifying the paper
sanctifying the moment.

I want to write
one line
of poetry
perfect
as a bough of Forsythia

pirouetting, Ikebana-like,
in a slender, silver beaker.

But
all that stutters
from my sorry pen

is chicken soup and matzo balls.

Stafford as Companion. Dolphin as Mentor.

a voice...so intimate and collective
at once. How did he do this?
An intense awareness of presence
and absence...
He dug in the ground. He picked
things up and looked at them.
—Naomi Shihab Nye on William Stafford

Stripes toward the horizon. Deep navy.
Light turquoise. Navy. Aquamarine.
Navy. Poised exactly on the world's edge,
three triangular sailboats. Pocket
handkerchief size. Whipped cream foam
at the liminal edge of sand and sea.

She picks up the shell she just stubbed
her toe on; sheepishly holds it to her ear.
Feels a bit like those beach-walkers
who wear headsets all the time.
They're listening to the sound of the waves
crashing, she jokes to her sweetheart.

How can anyone bear to interfere?

There is so much. Digesting
just a morsel of what lies underfoot,
in the crystal clarity of today's water;
watching the school of sheepshead
do their zebra imitations; seeing
tiny shellfish burrowing back
into the sand as the wave recedes;
watching one pelican plunge,
one skimmer skim; being present
for two moments could overwhelm.

Aldous Huxley was right. We do filter.
For to be so alive means that you know
what you don't.

She watches a dolphin close to shore.
The dolphin breaks the ocean's surface
like a ballerina's hands in second position.
Gently leaves sight again barely causing
a ripple. In. Out. Languid. Grace itself.

This, she decides, is how to manage it.

The Work

Dark chocolate with chili.
Even better, dark
chocolate with sea-salt,
covering chewy caramel.

I groan with pleasure
when I eat.
Last night it was
spicy piri-piri chicken,
farm salad greens,
sweet grape tomatoes,
a Greek olive oil and the erotic
honey of white Balsamic vinegar.

It's the paradoxical. An elegant woman
who sounds like a sailor.
The mouth on her,
you might say, admiringly.
A loving mother who knows
to say no, to yell when needed.
A classics professor who smokes
cigars, drinks too much, is rumpled
and messy. People of deep faith
who flirt daily with doubt.

I dig for the dirt in the folks
I work with, as I do with myself.

The white double-doors to the room
where the work takes place
can only be closed if you pull them in
simultaneously. Brad exclaims every time:
they're perfect: it's the "both-and"
we talk about.

Jennifer (Jinks) Hoffmann

Who is Driving the Bus?

Acting without thinking is like thinking without thinking.
—Rabbi Jonathan Slater

It passes like *that,*
the proverbial blink
of an eye,
and almost all the time

someone else is driving
the bus, and you
are not even looking
out the window.

Oh, the waste—
How to jar ourselves
from the wasteland
of eternal beta waves

that occupy space
and remove us
from the moment:
the sharpness of the knife,

the crystalline drop of water
on the tomato,
containing its own universe
if we but look;

the sweetness of the red apple,
tartness of the green,
the groan of the old fridge
turning over in weariness.

There are breaths to be taken
in gratitude for life,
water to be blessed
as we wash our hands.

There is the pillow
beneath our head,
inviting release
into slumber,

the softness
of the flannel sheet,
extra warmth
on a cold night.

If only we could slip
into the slipstream
of this one ordinary
and blessed life;

instead we are caught
in thoughts which begin
and end, like the ouroboros
chasing and finding nothing.

Jennifer (Jinks) Hoffmann

HaMakom*

*(The) call to attentiveness...(emphasizes) that
a divinely guided life
requires ongoing commitment.*
                    —Michael Fishbane

The poem is based on a dream

There is a small chapel
in a clearing in the woods,
where time has invested
her entire savings.

The old pine seats
are rounded by years of prayer,
and the floors gleam golden
with sunlight, which pours
through large and generous windows.

The smell of lemon oil
and gladness, vases of garden roses
and lilac, the sounds of prayer-
books opening, pages and hearts
alive with gratitude—all
welcome the new day of praise.

Songs are sung in the small chapel
in a clearing in the woods,
every day of the year.
Voices—of men and women and children—
are lifted like butterflies, like lace
patterns in a doily, as they join
to make beauty from air.

Deer and foxes gambol together
around this small chapel
in a clearing in the woods.
This sanctuary, older than knowledge,
is the home of invitation and refuge.

Men and women and children
will come and go;
but the place, quiet as a rock,
holding all secrets,
remains.

HaMakom: Hebrew for The Place, one of the 72 names for God.

Jennifer (Jinks) Hoffmann

I Don't Believe in God

My wife complains a lot.
Mind you, two small children,
me working all those hours,
I don't blame her. Once,
I was driving along the Don Valley,
and a mattress was laying
right in the middle of the road.
I guess the young men driving
the other car didn't learn
good knots at Boy Scouts.
Mind you, I shouldn't talk.
My parents couldn't send me
to Scouts. I needed to help
in the store. I've done better
than they did. I almost own
this cab. When they came
from Pakistan they had nothing.
They don't have much, even now.

It was a bad winter this year.
Lots of snow. Icy too.
Once my car slid all over
the highway and ended up
in the opposite direction.
I don't believe in God, but something
saved me. My passengers too.
They were nice, didn't yell or shout
or anything. My parents came to Canada
with nothing. Look at me now.
A wife. Two kids. She complains
a lot. It's hard with small kids.

I get to work seven days a week.
Almost own this cab. Sometimes
I even bring Swiss Chalet
home for a treat. Maybe God
believes in me.

No Jackson Pollock

No amount of immersion
in the mystical soup of life,
no amount of longing and pleading,
no amount of praying,
produces anything other
than pedestrian phrases.
No swaths of violent,
seductive colours flung
from my longing pen.
The dearth of drama deafens.

Bribery, flattery, begging
have no effect, despite
dues paid in years of writing,
and thoughtful reflection.

While I long for phrases
like:
the pleated curtains of wind,
playing hopscotch
with mortality,
are pulled tightly against
her longing for...
or:
life was torn from tree-tops
and flung nastily at ivory towers
or:
a slight blanket of fog covered
the industrious downtown core;
ugly lights switched
allegiance and departed
with night's promise...

all I get is painstaking portraits
of dots, squares and circles,
alarmingly Vasarely in scope,
red after blue after green,
red after blue after green,
red after blue after green.

The Path

The soul is like an uninhabited world
that comes to life only when
God lays (God's) head
against us.
Translation of poem by Saint Thomas Aquinas.
—Daniel Ladinsky

I have tried
to align my life
with The Path,
though it has a nasty
way of jogging
and turning
without reason
or warning.
Consulting mystics,
and reading masters
of several faith traditions
has helped not at all.
But I believe
I may have found
a clue, even a guide,
though I know not
the wisdom intended.
Our Border Collie, Kerry,
crouches flat against
the kitchen floor,
brown eyes locked
with mine, whenever
I speak on the phone.

The minute I end the call,
she spins in frantic,
counter-clockwise circles,
yelping in ecstasy,
then once more
belly to floor, growls
till I place my face
against her black-and-white head,
close to the black patch
over her right eye,
which makes her look
like a cross between
Moshe Dayan and Sinbad.

Jennifer (Jinks) Hoffmann

The Grandeur of the Individual
in the Smallness of Life

Truth is truth. Mind-tangles and suffering are universal,
and the desire for happiness and the end of suffering
is also universal.

—Sylvia Boorstein

It may not be the mother,
always soft-spoken,
reading bedtime stories,
and serving green vegetables
to her children,
who gives us pause,
but the mother
whose patience has fled,
yelling at her kids,
then gathering them
in a group hug--
as she sobs in remorse.

It may not be two doctorates,
or tales of untold wealth
that pique our interest,
but the professor
who talks endlessly
about his passion
for organic farming,
or the CEO
who hasn't missed one game
of his son's losing baseball team.
Life is small. There is only
this moment and the next,
this person with brown eyes,
the next with grey hair;

this man who worries
whether his kid will be
as anxious as he is;
this woman teaching
her daughter piano.
Life is small.
There is only this person
and the next, this life
that speaks of longing now,
and gratitude tomorrow.

Life is small,
there are professors
and mothers and fathers,
children and pianos,
tomatoes and baseball;
life is small,
there is only now—
only a series of nows.

Perhaps the grandeur
is just showing up
and saying yes,
to this moment
and the next.

The Deep End

I am the soapstone,
You are the sculptor.
All I need is to be still
as Your deft fingers
carve, smooth, chip away
that which is not me.
It is difficult not to tremble.

I am a field
which needs to lie fallow
for the best growth
of future crops.
As You drive over me
tilling the ground of my being,
it is difficult not to tremble.

I am a peach tree,
a wedding bouquet of pink and lavender
blossoms. You tell me the pruning
ensures that next year and the next,
I will produce even more peaches,
luscious with juice.
It is difficult not to tremble.

I am a mandala sandpainting
created in hours of silent meditation,
by a Tibetan artist.
You are the Hand that turns
sand to dust.
It is difficult not to tremble.
I stand naked. Alone.
In a field as wide as the sky.
I look around longingly
for someone to say yes.
I stand alone. Naked.
It is difficult not to tremble.

Jennifer (Jinks) Hoffmann

Speaking of Wild Pigs

Buddha's words as he lay dying:
we must be a lamp unto ourselves.

This I know:
everything I know
with certainty
could fit
into an acorn-sized
doughnut
in the palm
of my hand.

Why the size
of an acorn,
why a doughnut?
you ask,
seeking enlightenment.

If I was pretending,
I would offer wise
counsel, suggest that
the acorn is mother
to the mighty oak,
and the doughnut
represents circles
of emptiness
and wholeness.

But I would be
pretending.

Acorn and doughnut
sprang fully formed
into this poem,
of their own volition.

They probably arise
from the same place
as do dreams.
Marie Louise von Franz
said dreams come
from the same place
as the wild pigs.

As for me,
I have no idea
about wild pigs,
acorns, doughnuts
and origins
of consciousness.
All I know
with *certainty*
could nestle noisily
in the palm
of my upturned hand,
leaving ample room
for the wisdom
of others.

But hark, it is time
to light my lamp.

Second Nature

What will I do if I discover
that all You really want
is for me to cut the crap
of talking and writing
endlessly
about You?

What if all You really want
is for me to be,
no kidding,
in the moment.

Just be present.
Here. Now.
Stop talking. Stop writing.
Just be. Watch the moment
or my breath,
or the ten-thousand things
that rise and fall away.

What if You want me
to be like Rumi,
to sit in silence
and listen
as You say be more silent?

What if You think
my endless in-breath out-breath
on the Tetragrammaton
is a waste of time?

What if all the talking
and writing and thinking
and reading and combing
through my dreams
and my life, is rubbish?

What if there is no You,
no nothing,
just the moment?

What if You're Buddhist?
That's an oxymoron,
You say impatiently.

Look here, God.
I'm Jewish. I should stop
thinking, writing, talking,
meditating, reading, combing?
Get real! It's my second nature.

Find your first nature, You growl.

Section 4:
Family and Friends

A Caesural Moment

The human being before us is a divine image
of life...inspired with earthly particularity.
                                    —Michael Fishbane

There are times—precious few—
so exquisitely alive with existence
that something elemental breaks

into your normal waking state.
You look around, startled.
There is nothing to be seen.

It's close to eleven. I'm reading
this French Canadian writer,
whose depictions of people and meals

evokes my passions for the mystery
of humanity and for food: the Chief
Inspector, a man, subtle and direct,

looks appreciatively at mushrooms,
garlic, basil and parmesan atop a plate
of steaming home-made pasta. I look

across the bed at my man. His Kindle has begun
its nightly descent. He drops and lifts it, pretending
he's absorbed in what he's reading.

His eyes are half-mast. I stroke his left arm—
I seem to do this most nights—and he turns
and gives a crooked smile. I'm torn between

lingering on him and reading, when suddenly,
it's one of those moments—
I feel as if I mustn't even breathe.

The air seems to enfold me as I am as still
as a sculpture. Any movement
is too much. My man and my book.

Now I turn slowly and gaze around the room,
nodding in reverence at the lamp's glow,
the silent television, the colourful fabric
our son brought from his trip to Africa.

Surely, I muse, God
is in this place
and I didn't even know it?

And then, he yawns loudly.

Sacred Conversation

You meet—

close the doors
to the other reality
and enter this one.

Meeting with this intention,
creates Sabbath.

It is like this with prayer.
You can say I sure hope
so-and-so gets better

or you can shut your eyes,
and hope becomes prayer.

The silence and the talking
become the lemniscate
that weaves back and forth

so that neither knows
where each begins or ends.

When you arise at the end
of such a meeting
drenched in kairos time

you walk differently
into a different world.

Jennifer (Jinks) Hoffmann

Marriage

We Raised Each Other...
....grew up together
—Terry Tempest Williams

Now he stalks seventy-seven
and I seventy-three.

We have tried to clean
the messes we made.

You can never erase
the damage, but perhaps

a lack of tidiness
is part of the wild beauty

we call life together.

I still don't know
how to talk about time

or death. All I do know

is to brown the onions first,
before adding the garlic
and chili peppers

for troffia ala olio.

Advice on How to Create a Good Enough Relationship

When the slings and arrows
ricochet between you,
always assume

you are the grit, not the pearl.
Especially when this
is not true.

When you're both sure
you're right,
you're both wrong.

When the silence between
you becomes filled
with your demons,

sing loudly
from your favourite opera.
Preferably in tune.

Get yourself a good sieve.
Be prepared to sit
on the kitchen floor often.

Patience for sorting
wheat from chaff
and clean finger-nails

are advised. Leave
your false teeth
in the glass beside

the bed. Don't drink
that water. Know that
you go around

the same track
forever. Pray like
the devil that you spiral

closer to centre.
At least occasionally.
Have one friend with large

ears and a small mouth,
with no opinions,
and the willingness to walk

long distances beside you.
When you repeat
yourself again and again,

when you growl
rather than speak
in a normal tone,

when you shut
your mouth and refuse
to open it for days,

assume someone else
has inhabited your body.

Together, watch a Monty Python
movie, and *A Fish Called Wanda.*
Know you have partnered with
your teacher.

Tear up this list.

The Mystery of Blue Eyes

For many years I thought
it was his blue eyes
or catholic intelligence,

perhaps his balanced
perspective on world events,
money, and groceries.

But as I look back I realize
it was his oddities, like the discovery
that placing his bedside radio

upside down caused it to play perfectly;
he also let slip that he was reading
Atlas Shrugged for the second time.

Who reads *Atlas Shrugged* even once?
I was oddly intrigued by his
left-handedness, and the fact

that he knew all the words
to the show-biz tunes; he sang
frequently, though out-of-tune. This happened

in the sunny days of the early 60's
when we didn't see
how the sun hid the blood

of the Black South Africans.
I tease him he didn't propose,
but that somehow our love decided

we had to marry and leave.
These days I still don't know
why my heart jumps

when I think of him; he is still
left-handed and frequently reads
absurdly long books; breathes noisily

through his nose, and frowns
when he practises show-biz tunes
on the piano. He seldom laughs at my jokes,

but I am determined,
and will not cease trying for
a guffaw. We know more now

about the blood, and have spent
our many years together in gratitude
for being able to raise our kids

in a country less temperate,
but one where they can bring
anybody home. As for my heart's

jumping, I've given up trying to understand.
Instead I find myself singing
lustily and out-of-tune whenever

I hear his key in the front door.

Shiva*

It's the third night.
She's only been gone
four days. It's winter—
brutal outside too.

We do not know
what to do
with ourselves,
and so resort
to pawing awkwardly

at the ground, like donkeys,
as we talk about restaurants

with people
we have just met.
Friends of friends.
How do you keen

with complete strangers,
who, in trying
to be kind,
pin you
to a corkboard
with words
and questions?

Jennifer (Jinks) Hoffmann

So we become
like butterflies,
eyes glazed,
delicate wings
frozen
in mid-flutter.

*Shiva: means seven in Hebrew and refers to the week-long
mourning period observed after a death.*

(On the event of Joan's, my sister-in-law's, death.)

Home

We decide to stay home;
forgo our usual vacation.
Canada can be decent
in the summer, we agree. We sit
outside on our weathered deck;
sweet, dusky bird-song bathes us.

We're eating a mainly vegetarian dinner.
Fresh Asian salad greens, a Greek
olive oil and a thick balsamic dressing.
Pasta with Swiss chard, mushrooms
and bok choy, sautéed in green garlic.
Italian Romano grated onto the pasta.
An Argentinian Malbec this time,
my sweetheart suggests.
A veritable world trip.

The vegetables courtesy of Farmer Dan.
Farmer Dan is our son. Life
has blessed us with three sons
and eighteen grandchildren.
In some homes it is not correct
to talk about how many grands
you have. We do, with relish.
We also casually mention
our seven great-grands.

Jennifer (Jinks) Hoffmann

Home was South Africa.
Sweetness, when we were kids,
was figs, peaches and plums
picked from the garden,
pap,* with onion and tomato gravy
shared with the Black people.
We called them servants.
Sweetness, when we were kids
was ignorance.

Home is where the heart is, they say.
What happens when you have two homes?
We don't have two hearts; just longings
for figs and peaches and plums,
for pap* and the sounds
of Black African music and dialect,
for the redness of the earth, and the vastness
of landscape; for the knowing
before the knowing
of the Sharpeville Massacre
when sixty-nine were mowed down—
for peaceful protest.
Police guns blazed. All that was left
to companion the sixty-nine pairs
of feet on red soil, was the sigh of dust,
seeking redemption.

pap; a stiff porridge made from maize.

One of Those Days that Could Break Your Heart

It's one of those days that could break your heart,
every which way. Spring is finally deigning
to flirt with us, and the tiny buds of the French Lilac
at the front door begin to uncurl from their tight-fisted
resentment of the bitter winter. They will probably blossom
in about two months. I send a quick prayer as I leave the house;
may full bloom not happen in July, when we're on vacation. Amen.
The aroma of French Lilac rivals Jo Malone's pomegranate.

I'm at Metro buying milk and cinnamon—it's the latest
health spice—and I see a geezer with a shock
of white hair looking around in confusion;
the Filipina store assistant walks behind him,
talking about rye bread. He nods blankly.
I bless them both in my heart and leave the store
with two full bags of groceries. I always buy more
than intended. I take the long way home
so I can cheer the Forsythia and tiny crocuses
which just two days ago burst into celebratory blossom.

Now I'm driving home from Sunnybrook, where Lin
has been in the ICU for over ten days.
It wasn't supposed to be like this. She did say,
when we took her for dinner to celebrate her 70th,
that heart surgery is always risky, but she was playful
and cavalier as she spoke. She usually is. One of her qualities
I love the most. Twelve hours on the operating table.

Jennifer (Jinks) Hoffmann

Sibelius' *Second Symphony* plays on the radio
as I drive home. The final movement. I don't know
what to do with my heart which soars in triumph
and longing, as the haunting theme keeps repeating.
I don't know how to manage my love for Lin and Greg,
her son, who has been *working* on his mom daily.
He is not the healer he tells me, but says he thinks
the meditations and his love serve her. I agree.

It's one of those days when the air is soft breath
in this moment, and a cold wind in the next;
when wisps of blue chased by white cottontails dance
across a generous heaven in one moment;
and black scowls of clouds take hostage
of the sky in the next. It's one of those days,
I tell you, when my heart insists on breaking open,
when, in the face of it all, I feel a little like those buds
of the French Lilac, unfurling in several directions,
going this way and that.

Open the Door

For Susie K.

Every single word
has valence.
Even a teacup
can sing.
Do not feel
important
just because
you're Picasso.
You can say
open the door,
and God
may walk in.

Make every piece
of nothing
the something
that is.

Jennifer (Jinks) Hoffmann

Grass Blades and Flies

...a feeling of tenderness so still and deep and warm
that it gilds every grass blade and blesses every fly.
—Germaine Greer

He has hairs on the tops of his ears,
but not too much on the top of his head.
He snorts when he eats soup,
and obviously was not taught
like little boats that go out to sea
I push my plate away from me.
He says *I'm right* too often,
even when, in your opinion, he is light years
from realizing that facts and opinions
are not even kissing cousins.
He's gained weight and his wattles hang;
he used to fill out his clothes just right.

But somehow, all of this disappears,
when he smiles slowly, tilting his head
to the left, when the skin around his nose
wrinkles just like his mother's did,
and even though you hated
his mother, your knees go weak.
He walks fast with his head forward and down,
and says your name like no-one else.

It's not even so much the nice things he does,
like coffee in bed on Sundays, or buying a good salmon
and grilling it just so, because you asked,
every drop moist. He's rather good
at fixing cupboards that suddenly get old,
and knows masses about world events and sport.

It's not even so much the nice things, but rather
the quirks that write his name in the heavens,
like the fact that his fingers look like bananas,
and his singing is so soft, you can barely hear it.
Even the fact that he looks increasingly
like Mr. McGoo as he squints at the crossword
in *The Globe*, and climbs the stairs at half-speed,
causes grass blades and flies in your vicinity
to be gilded.

Jennifer (Jinks) Hoffmann

There was a Time

The shadows are lengthening.
It is that time of day when boundaries blur–
between houses and their small lawns–
light and dark, daylight and dusk.
Tomatoes, beans, peas and basil reach lazily
towards the remaining wisp of sun.

The neighbourhood is not yet gentrified;
some have owned for over thirty years.
The wheels of the double stroller squeak;
WD 40 grandpa says as they push
the girls home from daycare.
Will you stay for supper? Maya asks.
Granny nods at grandpa.
The girls debate. Should they sing
ABCD or *Baa Baa Black sheep*?
Maya's voice is pure, sweetly in tune,
Clara's a beat or two behind.
She's good for a two-year-old
grandpa says. Granny nods.

It's Granny's special supper treat:
cheese omelettes, toast, melted butter.
The trick is to beat the egg whites separately,
she tells the girls with mock graveness.
The bath routine tonight will be special.
Yogurt containers, old shampoo bottles,
a plastic heart in the water, and granny
making her huge soap bubbles between
her thumb and index finger. The girls wear
pink and purple pj's. *My favorite colour,* Maya
says imitating some of the older girls in daycare.
Me too, says Clara, imitating Maya.

98

Maya lines up five dolls for a bed-time story.
Grandpa does all the voices of *Cat in the Hat:*
his specialty. Maya begins to sing *O Canada,*
her self soothing song. She's winding down.

She is a big girl now. Has a big girl bed.
Pink and purple flannel sheets with butterflies.
Her other Granny gave her the pink blanket
tucked in so snugly.

Granny looks longingly at the bed.
There was a time when she too
did not know of shadows or boundaries.

Section 5:
Roots

Hidden and Revealed

All my bones will speak
          —Psalm 35:10

Not just speak, but sing.
Sometimes with the aching
of a well-earned seventy-three
year-old body, more often
with the awe of awakening.

Sometimes I spin round
knowing I am not alone,
for the very air hums
with gratitude, and question
and answer become one.

I seldom see anything remarkable;
perhaps a leaf dancing
an adagio on the outskirts
of an ordinary oak, maybe another
seventy year old walking

behind me. There is nothing
to see. There is everything
to see. It is a little frightening
to walk in the world thus:
husks falling away, no longer
necessary.

Jennifer (Jinks) Hoffmann

But if I can stay the moment,
not run into some imagined
disturbance; if I can breathe
in unison with the breath of life,
if I can simply walk on,
I will not silence

my bones, and they will rise up
in chorus and proclaim
kadosh, kadosh, kadosh
Adonai tze'va'ot, melo kol
ha'artez kevodo*

* Holy, holy, holy all the world is filled with Your glory.

Lamed Vuvnik

*There is a myth in Jewish Mysticism that teaches there are always 36
holy men or women in the world. Nobody knows who they are, not even
they themselves. These holy people are thus hidden. The myth tells us
that it is because of their existence that God does not destroy the world.
Since none of us knows whether or not we may be a Lamedvuvnik, it
behooves us to lead a humble life, one dedicated to wholeness.*

He wore his nickname lightly;
maybe even then he knew
of life's affection for him. Did he also know
that his absence of striving
to be one of the boys, to be top
of the class, to be a stand-out in sports,
would make him a magnet for the girls?
He didn't seem to care much about this
either. At twelve he already knew
things. The Rabbi and an old lady
in the town claimed
he was simply in love with God.

Shtoonk,* his older sister would call,
clean up your mess. Sometimes he did,
sometimes he didn't. Shtoonk, his younger brother
would beg, throw some balls to me. Sometimes he would,
sometimes he wouldn't. He wasn't holy, just unusually
easy in his skin. He wasn't pious,
he just noticed things, and there was an odd
stillness about him, even when he played
the games twelve year olds do.

It was as if he were in alignment with some thread
between heaven and earth, as if he had an ear
attuned to wind and birds, as if he were listening
to something others could not hear. Sometimes
he was helpful to his mother, sometimes
he wasn't. There was just something about him.

His father, a gentle, ineffectual man,
went to synagogue every week.
He, too, said Shtoonk was in love with God.

*   *   *

In their fifties, some women from the town
reminisce at Susie's diner.
They discover they all dream
of him from time to time,
even those who don't usually dream.
They decide he had something, even at twelve.
They muse about the origin of his nickname
to no avail, and conclude it's odd
they all dream about him.
They also discover, upon comparing notes,
they always wake up happy when they do.

As for Shtoonk, turns out he has his own
modest garden company. He's humble—
it's called *anavah* in Hebrew, humility;
taking your right place; not too much,
nor too little. He's still married to Janey,
who was one of those girls who didn't stand out
either. They have three kids, all of whom
seem unremarkable, like Shtoonk.
Reasonably happy and healthy, the women say.
The family still lives in the small town.

His father died in his nineties. He blessed Shtoonk
after a fashion just before he died. We should have called
you by your right name, Jacob, his father said.
Shtoonk just smiled and blessed his father back.

* *Shtoonk is Yiddish for stinker, usually considered to be a detestable person.*

Jennifer (Jinks) Hoffmann

Ein Od Milvado *

*Everything depends on one's focus or attention. To lose attention is to
slip into (mindlessness) that disregards the vastness of
existence...(and) betrays God.*

—Michael Fishbane

You think your joy arises
from the unfolding tableau
of the scrawny tawny kitten toying
with the honey-roasted peanut butter
on the cracked blue Delft saucer
left lazily on the linoleum floor
of the kitchen; by the sun slanting
through softly opened white curtains;
by the kettle whistling—a harbinger
of lemon ginger tea; and by your one-year old
screaming in delight while throwing
plastic containers from her playpen.

* There is None else.

Mount Sinai Morning Meditation

Construction clamor nearby.
A siren on Ben Yehuda.
A dog barks without cessation.
Teens talk loudly. A man,
wearing sunglasses, drums
with a strange urgency.

Yet in the clamour
a silence so lush
it is hard to breathe.

Perhaps in the silence
You are praying
we remember that
we always stand at Sinai,
that each of us is only one letter
of the Torah, written
in this place, not that.

Perhaps in the silence
You are praying
that we do not try to change
another's letter
to be the same as ours,
that we do not try to be
in a different place
in the Holy Book.

If we succeeded
there would be
no Torah.

Jennifer (Jinks) Hoffmann

Perhaps You are praying
we know the silence is filled
with Your love songs.
Perhaps You are praying
we keep reading
and re-reading
the original score.

Perhaps You are singing
our names, and asking
us to remember—
that to say a person's name
is to know them.

Be a Living Psalm

It matters not.
The dialogue and arguments
are not worth
the air you expend.

Rather, pick up the empty
beer bottle and rumpled
week-old newspaper
from the sidewalk.

Stop, for just that moment
as you slice the peach
with a serrated knife.
Two drops of juice.

Look into the watery eyes
of the homeless man;
they may or may not
be vacant.

Hold the hand of your partner
of fifty years, listen
to the faint whistle of air
through his nostrils.

Be patient with your impatience
with your aged Mother;
know she hates
you, too, at times.
Lift your eyes to the ballet
of eagle and wind, a wind
that can sometimes send
roof tiles and tree limbs flying.

Jennifer (Jinks) Hoffmann

Slice the radish paper-thin,
spread it fan-like around
the white plate. Bless the avocado
before you eat it.

Know that life shakes herself
awake each day, that random
pieces fall into your lap.
Your job is to hold praise

and lament with equal regard.
Your job is to be a living psalm.

Reflection on Psalm 90

The mist lifts
  several times
    each day

if we could but notice.

And then, before our eyes,
   not rubies or pearls
      but stones cast in dusty clay

which we can grasp
   with our ordinary hands
      to continue building

our ordinary homes.

Not the words and the words,
   not the images and the images
      not the theories and the theories

but the work
   of our hands
      firmly found.

Anything

Anything can be anything. That's mysticism for you.
—Rabbi Lawrence Kushner

It's just dinner with your husband
and your sister, her treat this time.
Lamb shanks and grilled sardines and rapini.

It's just a long table of thirty-somethings,
one making an impassioned speech,
and only three or four listening.

It's just that you could be the speaker,
or the pretty woman not listening,
or the good-looking man she leans toward.

It's just getting home before eight-thirty;
time to see the early news, and nothing,
unusually, is devastating tonight.

It's just getting into bed early
because your throat's a bit sore,
and spring is extra cold this year.

It's just the brown and cream blanket,
knitted by your mom some forty years ago,
and feeling cosy and safe.

It's just reading about ordinary people
and their dogs, and pea soup for dinner,
and snow on the village green.
It's just putting your book down and saying
I need to speak to you. I don't know
if I can find the words...

Do you ever get the feeling
there is something bigger,
and because of this,

everything feels just a little different?
The same and different. Slower
and better. Maybe even happier.

The same and different. *The dinner,* you say,
those folks at the table next to us;
even the tiny bones in the sardines.

And when he says *what do you think this is?*
You mumble *God,* and suddenly feel
sheepish and tearful, and wonder
if you should have said anything.

Hospitality

Let us, like Abraham,
peel back the flap of our tent,
quietly sweep the sand
from the entrance.

Let us slowly pour the wine,
watching in wonder as light sparkles
through red-gold liquid
splashing into the pewter beaker.

Let us remember a time
long ago, not long ago,
when we, too old, too young,
too foreign—were the strangers.

Let us see that we are blessed,
as we tear a hunk of still-warm bread,
and silently or with song,
share our ordinary abundance.

Let us hold the other close,
in our arms or in our hearts,
wordlessly, or with words,
recognizing we serve the Source of Life.

Let us know that love is stronger
than fear, than difference, than death.
Let us do what it takes
to be fully human.

Eden

In Hebrew Eden means delight or pleasure.

And so it goes—
this moment hands the baton
to the next, and the dominoes
fall...at times with grace,
more often, not—

The days move on, nothing
stopping them.

A lavender hedge borders
a mandala of rose bushes
at the edge of the garden.
A single lilac rose stands
in a vase on the old pine table
in the kitchen. Paradise,
it is told, is known
by its distinctive
aroma.

Songs are sung, glasses lifted,
light amplifying the legs
on the red wine dancing
down the sides of the huge goblet;
a study in contrasts with
the stillness earlier that day,
of downward facing dog,

Jennifer (Jinks) Hoffmann

where silent
breaths were offered
in honest devotion.
Now juices on almost blue steaks
are kissed, and children,
bedded for the night,
hum to their dreams,
in restful abandon.

This moment it is this,
the next, that;
and before you can say
limburger cheese, questions
about headstones
will be raised.

Noble pledges for mindful living
have no effect on dominoes
falling. Promises to cherish
friends and summer
are not worth
the breath they cost.

Truth is we seldom
remember we live
in Eden,
until the doors threaten
to clang shut in silence.

Faithfulness, not Faith

*… In order to come fully to the encounter with whatever gives
ultimate meaning, in order to really wrestle with the Angel,
one must be a free agent, not defined by another…*
—Marilyn Sewell

They branded her. A blue number.
On her forearm. Like cattle.
But though she watched her entire family
rise to the heavens, angry plumes
of unwilling sacrifice, her fire
of faithfulness stayed rooted
to the ground, centred
in her fierce absence of faith.

She wore her number like a flag,
unfurled to her commitment
to the spirit of life, and to the new
family she created in a new land.
She wore her number as a vow,
an indelible mark of truth

acquired in her encounter with evil.
The antidote—which she taught
schoolchildren, doctors, nurses,
university students, anybody
who would listen—was to know
that, under it all, was one heart
beating. Love could triumph, she taught,

but only if we stared down
hatred and violence,
only if we refused to stand down
when we needed to stand up
and be counted. The antidote
to evil, this frail, tough old woman
insisted, was to wrestle it.

She never called anything *God,*
but faithfulness to her family,
and to her call to unmask evil,
blessed the world
with the spirit of life.

Only her English was broken.

Belief in God

I am asked if I believe
in God? I say I believe
in Maples which know
how to bud at the end
of a weary winter;
in the impatience
of the female swallow
calling to her partner.
I say I believe in crocuses
that push through
eager soil, in young farmers
who seed tomatoes in basements
in winter's waning days. I say
I believe in school-children
who organize bake sales
and who proudly announce
they have raised one hundred
and seven dollars to send
to school-children in Haiti.
I say I believe in the mother
who, after a wretched night
of very little sleep, croons
as she feeds her children
oatmeal. I say I believe
in people who argue
that there are two or more sides
to the Middle East debacle,
and who cheer the woman
who carries a Torah
to the Wall in Jerusalem.
I say I believe in heeding
our very lives as teachers:
our moments of unease,

our dreams, and our difficulties
in relationships, as gifts of guidance.
I say I believe in silence
as well as music, that I know
for some, stillness is God,
while for others, God is the hallelujah
reaching the heavens.
I say I believe in love,
although, I say, sometimes
people get mixed up about love.
I say I believe in everything
anyone says is God,
except, I say, if they harm themselves
or others in God's name.
For I believe if there is a God,
that God would desire deep respect:
for ourselves and for others.

Do I believe in God? I am asked.
I say I am not too crazy about beliefs,
for when they are held without kindness,
there can be a mess of trouble.
And as for God, I say, the jury,
as far as I can see, is still deliberating.
But in the meantime, I say,
let's roll up our sleeves.

The Sand-Coloured Homes of Jerusalem

We can be cheerful and loose and jazzy in the face
of whatever life throws our way. Cheerfulness is a choice.
Happiness happens to you.
                                        —Garrison Keillor

It's not easy to be cheerful and loose
and jazzy, when missiles and rockets
fly between Israel and Gaza.
Too many of our beloveds
live in Israel: Devorah Leah,
our youngest grandchild, her fourteen
brothers and sisters, her nieces
and nephews, her mom and dad;
other relatives and friends.

But cheerfulness is a choice,
so I choose to remember
the faces of our beloveds,
the laughter we have shared;
I choose to pray for peace,
for all corners of the Middle East;
I choose to think of falafels,
and pita and humus, of friendly vendors
in the Arab section in the Old City;
I think of the sand-coloured homes
soaring on the hills of Jerusalem.

Jazziness feels a little far-off,
but if I look in my heart,
I may find God's hammock.
God rests there in the odd moments
between crises.

Jennifer (Jinks) Hoffmann

Now I Know Why I Sing When I Walk

Sing to God a new song
                    —Psalm 33:3

The melodies
bequeathed me—
I'dor vador,
generation unto generation—

deserve the voice of an angel,
so that my longing
be lifted up like Jacob's ladder,
giving song to what I know
I don't know.

In my heart there is one
with a violin so pure,
each string sings
when the wind weaves
even slightly.

And all I can do is hum tunelessly,
over and over, as I walk
my daily worship,
greeting
the sky.

Worship in S'fat

The absurd hum of the old refrigerator
and the drip of the tap which refuses
to be silent—unless you position the faucet handle
just so, slightly left of centre—
cannot drown out the mountains
proclaiming Your glory.

I think it is often like this:
the surface and the deep structure.
I think it is all You,
mountains in chorus, fridges and taps.
But sometimes humming and dripping
prevent us from hearing
even the hallelujahs of mountains.

Silver coloured olive leaves sway
in this morning's breathy wind
like Chasids shokheling on Shabbos.*
For a second, the wind ceases
and everything holds its breath.
Such reverence is almost too much
to bear.
Perhaps we should cover our eyes
like they do, when they pray
the Shma.....**

* Ultra-Orthodox Jews swaying to and fro in prayer on the Sabbath.
** Shma Yisrael, the centerpiece of the morning and evening Jewish
prayer service is considered the holiest prayer by many. It literally
means "hear, oh Israel."

Jennifer (Jinks) Hoffmann

Yirah*

All of Buddhist teaching in three simple words:
not always so.

—Suzuki Roshi

The hiccup between
here and there
now and then

is less

than a full breath
when you know

you cannot trust
your ground,

when you know

there is no-one,
no thing,

between you,

your life and death.

When you stop,
there is nothing

to do
but be aware of
how damn exquisite
how damn awful
it all is.

* Awe/fear/awareness

You Cannot See the Face of God and Live

It's impossible to keep life
at bay, to order it neatly,
funnel it through narrow slots,
like those on a child's pinball machine.
Days wake up and seem to decide,
of their own accord, to drag you
along for the ride wherever they go.
This is the inevitable part.
All you get to decide
is whether to go along
kicking and screaming, or to look
for interesting morsels, like tiny,
wild strawberries hidden in the cleft
of the same rock that shielded
Moses, when God passed by.

Epilogue

It's All God, Anyway.

It's not so much...
... this book in my hand—
or in yours—
the poems that passed
the finish line;
what people say;
or even life and death.

What matters most
is how the book,
the poems,
what people say,
and even life and death,
bring me closer
to God...
... when I ask
what now, my Love?

Forever. Amen.

Acknowledgements

In South Africa, the country of my birth, there is a word, *Ubuntu,* which means compassion and humanity, but is often translated to mean "I am who I am because of you."

I will acknowledge both those people who have been instrumental in helping me birth this book, and also those who, because they are important in my heart, are a part of my spiritual life. My poetry is simply a reflection of my spiritual life.

This book is the result of a request from my youngest son Daniel, who asked me to create a collection of some of my favourite poems. "So I can have them when you're gone," he said. I loved that he named that I would one day die. Dan asks the best questions and challenges me in just the right way. Little did either of us imagine the writing of the book would intensify my psychospiritual journey in a way that would be quite transformative.

My second son Glen is a fine writer and thinker. We share a passion for reading and writing. I cherish his honesty. My oldest son Eli is a devout man, and follows a dynasty of Judaism called Bobover Hasidism. I am deeply grateful to him for his faith, his fine intelligence, and for all I learn about my own religion through him. My sons are my teachers, each one so different from his brothers. My love for them is a bedrock of my life.

I am greatly indebted to my beloved parents Barney and Judy Davidoff, both of whom died much too early. From my dad I received the gifts of humour, empathy, consideration, and fear. From my mom, vitality, spirit, engagement, and impatience. I was both blessed and wounded by who they were. And the wounds were just as important as the gifts, for they compelled me to seek healing and ultimately a life lived in relationship with the divine.

My sisters Vicki and Sue teach me and make me laugh. We cry together, too. They are blood-and-soul sisters.

Jason Ranek, my poetry editor, has taught me an enormous amount about writing poetry, and also about living a spiritual life. Our relationship is sacred to me. We laugh a lot at ourselves, one another and life.

The call from within to persevere with this book has been hugely supported by my Jungian analyst Bob Gardner, my Toronto spiritual director Maureen McDonnell, and Rabbi Avruhm Addison, my Philadelphia spiritual director.

The four women with whom I do spiritual friendship exchanges—Laura Goldman, Suzie Kaufman, Pam Lauer, and Linda Zelizer, are all spiritual directors and beloved companions.

Anna Miransky and Diane Millis are beloved creative writing partners. My engagement with each of them is life-giving.

I must make special mention of Michael Fishbane's book *Sacred Attunement*, which I have read three times and which is a source of great inspiration. Michael has been most generous in his responses to some of my poems.

My beloved friends of over 50 years, Ruth and Stan Swartzman and Lin and Alan Judelman, are like family to me. Our love and closeness has grown immeasurably through Lin's medical crisis.

Brenda Greenberg, Merle Soldin, and my sister-in-law, Joan Hope, died well before their time. They are still very alive in my heart.

I am very blessed to have a wide circle of loving, encouraging friends and family. All of these people have been interested in, and supportive of me, as I have walked this path making my childhood dream come true: Barbara Bobrow, Nicki and Gerard Closset, Victoria Cowan, Stan and Rhoda Fischer, Miriam Frey, Ruth Gilbert, Aviva Goldberg, Lucinda Hage, Terry Hershey, Kristen Hobby, Marion and Jack Hoffmann, Katie Isbister, Delia Julian, David Liedl, Leila Nathans and Len Polsky, Lorna

Poplak, Judy Posner, Jerry Robbins and Christina McKenny Robbins, Stan and Jill Segal, Marion Soloway, Judy Viorst, Nick Wagner, Emily Wichland. My three daughters-in-law, Ilana, Medina and Terri are also loving and encouraging friends. Many thanks to Lisa Browning, for her warmth and generosity in the publishing of this book.

I acknowledge and honor the people I have worked with, as a psychotherapist and spiritual director, over many years and at the present time. In any relationship where wholeness is the goal and consciousness the vehicle, both are transformed. I am blessed and privileged by this work.

My eighteen grandchildren and seven great-grands, a source of enormous delight, love, and just plain amusement, are a rich aspect of my spiritual life. I will not mention them by name, for that could create another book.

Of course, the greatest acknowledgment goes to Alan, my husband. Alan has been a mirror to all the ways I am called to wake up and to grow. Mystery has had a hand in our relationship from the beginning. I tell him that our marriage is a kind of test tube where consciousness is incubated. A kind of alchemical container where we are each called closer to wholeness. He is my most profound teacher, simply because of who he is. His love and interested support for this book are incalculable. My love for him continues to bring me to what I call my "God-tears," frequently.

About the Author

I believe deeply that creativity is essential for a successful and fulfilled life. People frequently make the mistake of thinking that creativity needs to be poetry, painting, sculpture. Something praiseworthy. Creativity is much broader and more wonderful for me, and issues from engagement with the wisdom and guidance within us. Living creatively means doing something with the energy that is the source of your life. It can be as simple as spending time in making a salad as beautiful and nutritious as possible. It can be rollerblading. Walking in your neighbourhood mindfully and looking for beauty. Taking the time to listen to what comes from within and being guided by it is the way to go. Intentional time to give voice in some way to the spirit of life within.

—Jennifer (Jinks) Hoffmann, July, 2016

Jennifer (Jinks) Hoffmann and her husband Alan left South Africa and moved to Toronto, Canada in 1966, where they live for most of the year. They have three sons, eighteen grandchildren, and seven great-grandchildren. Jinks is a retired psychotherapist, and is currently a spiritual director in private practice. Alan and Jinks have a winter home in Marco Island, Florida, where Jinks' contemplative life quadruples. Jinks is the poetry editor of *Presence: An International Journal of Spiritual Direction,* and was on the Coordinating Council of Spiritual Directors International from 2008-2014. Her primary ways of listening for the voice of the Beloved are through dreams and poetry, through life's wonders, and when she messes up.

Spiritual Directors International has published a great deal of Jinks' poetry, and also her prose, in the journal *Presence* and in the *Listen* and *Connections* publications. SDI also has published several of her poems on their annual bookmark.

Jennifer (Jinks) Hoffmann

Much of Jinks' poetry and some of her prose has been published in the literary supplements of *Canadian Jewish News*, in newspapers in Florida, in synagogue bulletins, in *Refresh: A Journal of Contemplative Spirituality*. Her poems and essays have appeared in books by Janet Ruffing, Michael Crosby, Diane Millis, and *Numinous*, an online poetry magazine. The Israeli website *Cyclamens and Swords* has published some of her work, as has *Voices Israel*. Her poems have also appeared in Terri Hershey's online weekly column, *Sabbath Moments*. In 2006, the chapter Poetry and Spiritual Direction appeared in the book *Jewish Spiritual Direction: An Innovative Guide from Traditional and Contemporary sources,* Ed. Rabbi Avruhm Addison and Barbara Breitman.

Testimonials

Our job is to be a living psalm, Jinks observes, and this luminous collection of poetry points the way. Hoffmann's work will transport you to another realm while rooting you more deeply wherever you dwell. Entrust your journey to this gifted teacher and beloved guide. Her verse will enliven your days and expand your heart.

—Diane M. Millis, PhD, spiritual director, teacher, and author of *Deepening Engagement: Essential Wisdom for Leading with Purpose, Meaning, and Joy* **and** *Conversation—The Sacred Art*

It's All God, Anyway is a collection of prayerful poems that invite us to see the mysterious, loving unity that underlies all of reality. Hoffmann adroitly locates this sacred unity in the universe's multiplicity, which she offers us in graphic, moving detail. She extends her hand to readers of this heartfelt volume, taking us on a journey that moves and changes us.

—Rabbi Jacob Staub, Professor of Jewish Philosophy and Spirituality at the Reconstructionist Rabbinical College

Whenever I read Jinks I learn something. But I do not read Jinks' poetry only for instruction. I savor these poems because they open windows in my heart and soul. And because they make me smile. These are poems to experience, because they are invitations to see and celebrate, to taste gladness and delight, to embrace and be embraced by the presence of God and the sacred in the exquisite and unadorned present moment; yes, even in the shmutz. A great reminder that the unvarnished ordinary is the vessel of the holy fullness of life.

—Rev. Terry Hershey, Protestant Minister, dad, garden designer, wine lover, and author of *Soul Gardening and Sanctuary: Creating a Space for Grace in our Life*

This book invites you into a sacred conversation between Jinks and her ever present God, in the ordinary and the everyday---on the windy beach, in her dreams, in the smile on her granddaughter's face. Jinks has the courage to keep fronting up, to stay still in the dark spaces, knowing there are gifts to be gleaned.

The poems fill you with a joy that makes you feel understood---as if someone has seen into your heart and read its lines.

This book places inner work as the most important work we can do. The work is subtle, difficult and relentless, but I see the fruits of this work in the extraordinary person of Jinks. She delights in the work of others, her love and understanding are endless and she is the most self aware person I've ever met.

—Kristen Hobby, spiritual director, retreat leader and meditation teacher, and author of *Nurturing a Gentle Heart,* which explores spirituality for pre-schoolers

In 2001, I was blessed to meet the poet and person that is Jennifer (Jinks) Hoffmann. To quote her own words, her verse, born of exploring the God-pumps of life, tears your heart open while leading you to a place where the hidden and visible meet. Jinks helps you recall what your heart knows but has forgotten: that the rush of mystery frightens a little, that we are called to love not only when life is gentle.

If you open the door to the worlds contained within this book's covers chances are good that indeed… God may walk in.

—Rabbi Howard Avruhm Addison, PhD. Associate Professor for Instruction, Temple University. Director, Jewish Spirituality Program. Graduate Theological Foundation